# ARE YOU "THERE"
## - Where GOD wants you to be?

Unless otherwise stated, all scripture quotations are from the *King James Version* of the Bible.

1st printing

*Are You THERE – Where God Wants You To Be?*

ISBN 0-9791654-0-7

Copyright 2006 by Kevin E. Wright

Published by Word of Faith Christian Center-MS
4890 Clinton Blvd.
Jackson, MS 39209
www.wofcc-ms.com

All rights reserved

Printed in the United States of America

Reproduction of content or cover, in whole or in part without the express written consent of the Publisher is prohibited.

# ARE YOU "THERE"
## – Where GOD wants you to be?

### Kevin E. Wright

*Word of Faith Christian Center - MS*

*Jackson, Mississippi*

# Dedication

I dedicate this book to my loving wife and best friend, Leslie, who keeps me inspired and encouraged to carry out God's callings on my life; to our five children, Joshua, Stephen, Melissa, Daniel and Micah who are the joys of my life; to my spiritual parents, Bishop Keith A. Butler and Pastor Deborah Butler who are my mentors, and to whom I will always be grateful; and to my parents Mr. and Mrs. Earl Wright and Mr. and Mrs. Woodrow Hughes, the best parents in the world. Thank you for being "there" for me.

# Contents

Introduction                                        9

The Right Place at the Right Time                  13

What's Keeping You From Getting "There"?           19

Let God Direct Your Steps                          27

Find Your Purpose in Life                          39

How Do You Get "There"?                            45

# Introduction

Those who know me have heard the story a thousand times about my move to the South. I grew up in Detroit and began serving the Lord as a teenager. I joined Word of Faith International Christian Center with Bishop Keith A. Butler in the early developmental stage of the church. I worked my way up through the ranks, so to speak, doing whatever I could put my hands to do. I was the youth pastor, taught Bible classes; you name it, I did it. The church grew and I eventually became Bishop Butler's assistant pastor.

Then one day, Bishop Butler called me into his office and told me of his plans to start a new church in Jackson, Mississippi, and that I was to pastor it. Well, I was stunned. I had heard so many things about Mississippi, and none of them were good. I had seen the movie *Mississippi Burning* and had talked with other preachers who said that Mississippi was a "preacher's graveyard." They said the people there had a slave mentality and that is why they moved from there. I gathered data on the state and looked at the demographics. It didn't impress me. I wanted to go someplace big, like

Texas.

In my mind, because of all I had read and heard, I had stereotyped the state, just like people stereotype Detroit as being a city riddled with crime. Some of what I read was true. Certain things did happen here, and I could have gone somewhere else. However, I would not have been where God wanted me to be. I may have been blessed, but not like I am here, in the perfect will of God. We cannot let people, the media, or circumstances get us off course. As Christians, our number one job is to be where God wants us to be, doing His will, and bringing glory to His name. That is why I decided to write this book, to encourage you to seek God first, and everything else will be added to you.

## Chapter 1

# The Right Place at the Right Time

Are you "there" - where God wants you to be? The blessings of God are positional. Many Christians are not where they should be to receive God's best. They are at the wrong place at the wrong time. Until you get "there" you will experience lack. For many, "there" could mean being in the right church. Are you at the right church? Are you attending the right college or university? Are you at the right place of employment? Are you in the right city? Are you where God wants you to be? You should not concern yourself with how and when. Your only concern should be, **where does God want you to be?** Focus on being at the right place at the right time.

The Prophet Elijah focused on being where God wanted him to be and God worked miracles through him. In I Kings Chapter 16, the Bible says that King Ahab did more evil in the sight of the Lord than any other king before him. Ahab considered it a trivial matter to marry Jezebel, and worship her god Baal. He even built temples for Baal in Israel. In I Kings Chapter 17, Elijah let Ahab know that God was displeased with his waywardness and would punish his people with a drought. God then told Elijah to go to the brook Cherith. There he would drink from the brook, and the ravens would feed him in the morning and at night. Elijah went and stayed by the brook as the Lord told him. The brook was Elijah's "there." It was "there" by the brook that provisions were made for him.

After nearly a year, the brook dried up, and the Spirit of God came to Elijah and told him to go somewhere else. God will always forewarn you about something that is about to happen. God is always talking to us, but we are not always listening. God always has something to say, but the problem is on the receiving end. That is why it is so important for us to tune in. Life is all about making adjustments and tweaking our lives. If you trust in

God, in times of drought you will be satisfied.

## *Blessings Are Waiting On You*

God told Elijah to go to another place and a widow would help him. Notice the widow was already there gathering sticks, just as the raven was already waiting at the brook. They were already "there" waiting for the prophet. The blessings of God are waiting on you. The manifestation is already there, but it's up to you to get "there" - where God wants you to be. "There" is where God's supernatural provision will be. Where there is a vision, there will always be provision. The provision is there, waiting on you. However, too many times, we concern ourselves with wondering how or when something is going to happen. That is not our job. Our job is to get "there" - where God wants us to be.

## *There Are Different Phases in Life*

God told Elijah to go to another place. After some time, God will give you more instructions to do something different. He may tell you to go to this city, change careers, start a business, do this or do that, because where you are has dried up. You have to have enough spiritual sense to know when to move. Most people do not like change. But there are different phases in life and God can lead you to do something different. You can't get too comfortable.

## Chapter 2

# What's Keeping You From Getting "There"?

Let us look at how God led the children of Israel to the Promised Land, or their "there." The journey began in Exodus 13. Moses led them, but something kept them from getting there. It was *murmuring, complaining, doubt and unbelief.*

Exodus 14 says, the children of Israel whined, complaining that Moses had brought them out to the

Red Sea and now they were going to die. Moses stretched forth his staff, the sea parted and the children of Israel crossed over on dry land in the middle of the sea. When Pharaoh's Army came into the sea after them, the waters returned and destroyed the entire Egyptian Army.

In Exodus 15 they complained that Moses had brought them out there and they were going to die of thirst because the water was bitter. The Lord showed Moses a tree. When he threw the tree into the water, it made the water sweet. But they didn't stop there. In Exodus 16, they murmured again at Moses saying that they were going to die because they did not have anything to eat. So supernaturally God rained bread from heaven for the people. But they went on and on murmuring and complaining.

God was with them and He led them with a cloud by day and a pillar of fire by night. Their clothes never wore out. Yet the Bible says they wandered in the wilderness for 40 years. I wonder how many of us are still wandering in the wilderness, trying to get "there"? We do not want to wind up like the children of Israel, wandering for 40 years and then dying in the wilderness, never carrying out the will of God, never getting "there" - where God wants us to be. If only we would stop murmuring and complaining and having doubt and unbelief. Just focus on getting "there," where God wants you to be.

## *Don't Let It Go to Your Head*

Other behaviors that will keep you from getting

"there" are anger and pride. Remember the story about Naaman in *II Kings Chapter 5*? Naaman was the captain of the Syrian Army. The Bible says he was a great and honorable man. He was a mighty man of valor, but he was a leper. Naaman found out the Prophet Elisha in Israel could heal him of leprosy. So he traveled to Israel to the prophet's house. Rather than greeting Naaman himself when he arrived, Elisha sent his assistant out to tell him what to do. His instructions to Naaman were to go and dip seven times in the Jordan River. Understand, **Naaman's "there" was the Jordan River.** He would receive his healing of leprosy if he would just go "there." "But Naaman was wroth, and went away," according to *II Kings 5:11*. We don't talk like that nowadays. We don't say "I'm wroth."

He went away upset, in a rage.

Naaman continues talking in *II Kings 5:11*. He said, *"Behold, I thought..."* He became concerned with trying to figure out how it was going to happen. His thoughts probably were, "I thought the prophet would come and wave his hand or do whatever he does to heal people." You have to remember; they are not the ones healing people anyway. And besides, who told Naaman to think? Our job is not to do the thinking. Only God is all-powerful and all-knowing. That's why He is El Elyon, The Most High God. God said to get "there." In Naaman's case, he was to go to the Jordan and dip seven times. But Naaman was proud. He wanted to wash in one of the rivers of Damascus. After all, they were a lot cleaner than the Jordan. So he went away angry and still a leper.

It took Naaman's servant to talk some sense into him. The servant asked Naaman, if the prophet had told him to do something big, would he have done it? He reasoned, how much more then should Naaman do this small thing and go wash in the Jordan. I wonder why the Lord chose the Jordan. Perhaps it was because Naaman had so much pride. That is what happens often among leaders, pastors, and politicians. We have to be so careful with being prideful.

*Proverbs 16:18* states, *"Pride goeth before destruction, and a haughty spirit before a fall."* Never allow your name, title or position to go to your head. It will stop you from getting "there." Paul said in *I Corinthians 15:31, "I die daily."* Until you die to self, you will not find your "there." Zacchaeus, the rich tax collector, wanted to see Jesus. Being of short statue, Zacchaeus climbed a tree. He could have said, "I'm rich. I'm not climbing a tree to see anyone." Instead, he got rid of himself, his identity and got Jesus' attention. In the Garden of Gethsemane, Jesus could have used His power and called on the Father to send *"more than twelve legions of angels"* to rescue Him, *Matthew 26:53*. But Jesus was not thinking of Himself. He wanted to do the will of His Father, so the Scriptures would be fulfilled. What are you willing to do to get "there?"

## Chapter 3
# Let God Direct Your Steps

Do not bog yourself down with trying to connect the dots or figure out how to make something happen on your own. Don't make the mistake of thinking, "Let's see if I do this, then twist that and get this person to do this, and then I can get that." Who asked you to connect the dots? All God wants you to do is get "there." He will handle all the favor and anything else needed. When man takes you to the top, if you make one mistake, you're finished. But when God takes you to the top, man can't pull you down. I don't care what they try. They can sling dirt at you or talk about you, but it will work out in your favor.

When Bishop Keith A. Butler asked me to pastor a church in Mississippi, I wanted to go to New York or Texas. They do everything big in Texas, right? Yet, I would have gone to Texas and done everything small because I would not have been where God wanted me to be. It was a grand idea with good intentions, but what is most important is that you are where God wants you to be, in His perfect will. When you get "there," you will experience God's supernatural provision.

There is one other person I want to discuss before I explain how to get "there." I am sure you are familiar with the story of Jonah.

Jonah Chapter 1 begins:

> *1 Now the word of the LORD came to Jonah the son of Amittai, saying,*
>
> *2 Arise, go to Nineveh...*

**Nineveh was Jonah's "there,"** not Mississippi, California, Samaria or England. God told Jonah to go to Nineveh.

> *2 ...that great city, and cry against it; for their wickedness is come up before me.*
>
> *3 But Jonah rose up to flee (or run) to Tarshish from the presence of the LORD...*

God told Jonah to go to Nineveh, but he went somewhere else. Jonah had his reasons for not going, которое did not justify why he chose not to obey God. The Bible describes Nineveh as "an exceeding great city." It was large, the thriving capital of Assyria, centrally located on the eastern banks of the river Tigris, between the Mediterranean Sea and the Indian Ocean. Nineveh was an important traffic circle for commercial means, allowing wealth to flow into the city from many sources.

Jonah refused to go to help people he hated. No one can say for sure why Jonah hated Assyria, but the book of Nahum gives us an idea. Nahum describes the people of Nineveh as ruthless. They tortured and slaughtered people who opposed them. Therefore, Jonah had reasons to hate and fear Nineveh, but God loved them and wanted to save the city. Nineveh was Jonah's "there." God's plan had nothing to do with what Jonah thought. God wanted to use Jonah to bring about a change in Nineveh, and in the process change Jonah too. But Jonah was thinking for himself and tried to run away, doing the opposite of what God commanded. Listen, often your "there" is not where you want to go. How many times has God told you to go "there" – where you did not want to go? Maybe you thought, "I'm not doing anything." But understand, your going "there" is not necessarily just for you.

## *Your "There" is Not Just For You*

God told Jonah to go to Nineveh so the people could repent and God could cause revival in the city. Life is not about you. Remember Elijah? He could have said, "I'm not going to go to a widow and allow her to provide food for me." But God's purpose for sending Elijah to the widow wasn't just for him; it was also for her benefit. The widow was preparing what she thought would be the last meal for herself and child. However, because the prophet went where he was to go, not only was he blessed by the woman, but she was also because of her obedience to the Word of the Lord. She gave her last. She did not eat her seed. You can take your last $5 and say, "This is all I have. I might as well go get a Number 2 at Wendy's®." On the other hand, you can take that seed money and do what God tells you to do with it, meeting not only your needs, but also the needs of others. The Bible says the widow had a feast for days.

Your "there" is not just for you. God has greatly blessed my wife and me, and thousands of others because we went to **our "there" in Mississippi**. It was not just about us, but it was about the effect our obedience would have on others. It's about the big picture. Most people don't see the big picture. Jonah didn't see the big picture and refused to go to Nineveh.

Perhaps, God has been talking to you about doing something, but you have this preconceived notion about it. It's not about you. God needs us in every man's world. Most people base their decisions on how something will benefit them. God will have you do something that is way beyond you and bless you while you are doing it.

## *When You Don't Obey God*

Jonah decided not to go to Nineveh and went to Tarshish instead. Notice what will happen when you don't do what God tells you to do. Jonah boarded a ship going to Tarshish. The Lord sent a great storm. The men on board were afraid and began praying to their gods while Jonah was down in the lowest part of the ship fast asleep. They cast lots to find out who was the cause for the trouble. They knew someone on board had done something wrong. Even sinners will look at you strangely when you mess up. Your non-Christian friends or associates will tell you, "You need to go on back to church. You don't know how to do wrong right." The captain found Jonah and told him to get up and pray to his God so maybe He would spare their lives.

Jonah 1:17 tells us what happened to Jonah. *"Now, the LORD had prepared* (or He allowed) *a great fish to swallow up Jonah. And Jonah was in the belly of the fish three days and three nights."* It happened because Jonah did not go "there" where God wanted him to go. Instead, Jonah went where he wanted to go and did what he wanted to do. If you have that same attitude of, "This is the way I see it," you too will wind up in the belly of a great fish.

In Chapter 2, Jonah began to pray to God. He began crying in verse 2 and belly aching in verse 3.

> *3 For thou hadst cast me into the deep, in the midst of the seas, and the floods compassed me about: all thy billows and thy waves passed over me.*
>
> *6 I went down to the bottoms of the mountains; the earth with*

> *her bars was about me forever:*
>
> *7 When my soul fainted.*

Finally, in verse 10 of Chapter 2, Jonah gets it straight with God, *"And the LORD spake unto the fish, and it vomited out Jonah upon the dry land."* In other words, Jonah finally got his heart together, and the great fish vomited him back out toward "there" - Nineveh. What happened to Jonah will also happen to you when you are *not* "there" - where God wants you to be.

When you get out of place, you get into another man's or woman's lane. You are not to do certain things, yet you think you can. The anointing is not there for you when you are not where you should be. The anointing comes to lift burdens and it will take the toil and sweat out of work. If you are struggling all the time, it is because God did not tell you to do what you are doing. For example, let's say you believe God called you to be a hairstylist and you started with five customers. Then, ten years later, you have six customers. It appears that you are out of your calling because there is no increase. There is nothing wrong with being a hairstylist, but there should be an increase if you are doing what God has called you to do.

## Chapter 4
## Find Your Purpose in Life

Y ou have to find your purpose in life. You have to find your mission and stay there. As we move on to Jonah Chapter 3, isn't it great to serve a God of a second chance? The word of the Lord came again to Jonah the second time, telling him to go to Nineveh and preach as God commanded. I love verse 3, *"So Jonah arose, and went unto Nineveh, according to the word of the LORD. Now Nineveh was an exceeding great city of three days' journey."* Verse 4 says Jonah made it to the city in *a day's* journey. He quickly got to where God wanted him to be, "there" in Nineveh.

It didn't take Jonah long to figure out what he needed to do. It is sad to say it takes some people years. They wallow in stuff they should not be doing and are so unhappy. Have you met people who are unhappy? They have no joy. They may have a big house and other material possessions, yet they are still not "there," where God wants them to be. Why would you do something God did not tell you to do? Like Naaman, you're supposed to go to the River Jordan, not the Mississippi River! You're out there in the Mississippi River drowning and it looks bad.

Everyone can see you look uncomfortable and it is because you are not where you should be. But if you would just go to the Jordan River, you could do backstrokes; you would be gliding along swimming on top of the water. When you get to where God wants you to be, you won't have to struggle or try to make things work or happen because God is in control.

## *God Has a Plan for You*

The widow is already there gathering her sticks. The ravens are there. You just have to get with the program. When you are not where you should be, you will struggle. You will wear your little self out. I see Christians all the time, doing stuff they should not be doing. You can get in much trouble, being at the wrong place at the wrong time when God did not tell you to be there. Look at the trouble Jonah went through! Are you in the belly of the great fish? Naaman went away angry, and still a leper.

I know many people who do not want to hear it when you try to sit down and explain this to them. When you give them the word of the Lord, they leave your office angry. I may tell them, "You should not marry that person. Wait." However, they leave my office fuming. I may tell them, "Don't start that business yet; it's premature." They leave my office mad. Then they will say, "Aw, you're just trying to hold back my ministry." So what do they do? They flee to Tarshish. They go join another church where someone will put them in the pulpit and they can get one of the preacher seats. There is a set time for everything. God will speak to your leadership if you are submissive. I have seen people come and go because they do not want to wait. What happens is the devil will begin working in your life because you are out of season. Just as if you were wearing a wool hat when it is 100 degrees outside or wearing shorts when it is freezing cold. You will know when you are in your right place. The anointing will be there to help you.

*Word is a lamp unto my feet and a light unto my path," Psalm 119:105.* If you were in a dark room and lit just a small candle, that candle would light your way. The Word of God is a light. It will show you which way to go, left or right; do this or that. However, when you do not have the Word, you are going to bump into all sorts of stuff. I compare it to driving a car. If you drive through big potholes, over time you can destroy your car. Without the Word of God, you can destroy your life. That is why you need to follow the light. You need to follow the Word. Experience is a good teacher at the school of hard knocks, but the tuition is high. You cannot continue to get experience the hard way.

## *Follow the Voice of Your Spirit*

The next step is to follow the voice of your spirit. Look at *Proverbs 20:27, "The spirit of man is the candle of the LORD, searching all the inward parts of the belly."* God leads and guides us by our spirit.

*I Thessalonians 5:23* says, *"And the very God of peace sanctify you wholly; and I pray God your whole spirit and soul and body be preserved blameless unto the coming of our Lord Jesus Christ."* This scripture tells us the makeup of man. Man is a tri-part being. He is a spirit, he has a soul (that deals with your mind, will and emotions) and he lives in a physical body.

Someone once said the average Christian feeds his or her physical body three hot meals a day and one cold snack at night. They feed their spirit man one cold snack a day, around 10 or 11 at night. After they have done all they are going to do for the day, then they open their Bible thinking, "Let me see what God will say to me today," letting the pages fall to no particular scripture and began reading. "Let me see ...and Zerubbabel." Who in the world is Zerubbabel, and what does that have to do with them? So then, they put their Bible away and fall asleep because they do not understand. They do not grow at all. They are just religious. It was the religious people, the Pharisees and the Sadducees, who crucified Jesus. Today, there are still many religious people, having a form of godliness but denying the power of it. We are not religious. We are Christians.

The Bible lists several names for the spirit of man. The spirit of man is also the inner man and the hidden man. In *Ephesians 3:16* the spirit of man is the inner man. *"...To be strengthened with might by his Spirit in the inner man."* *I Peter 3:4* says the spirit of man is the hidden man. *"But let it be the hidden man of the heart, in that which is not corruptible..."*. This is how God leads you. Some might say it is your conscience. The conscience of a born-again believer is a safe guide. Others use the word heart, meaning the core or center. Follow your heart, the spirit of man, inner man, hidden man, or your conscience, and you will never go wrong.

## *Your Spirit Versus the Flesh*

You can always tell if it is your spirit man or the

flesh talking. The body's voice may say, "Give me that Twinkie® or give me a dozen Krispy Kreme® doughnuts." The voice of your spirit may quietly say, "No, don't do it." Whichever one you feed the most, will be the voice you will follow. Therefore, if you are only feeding your spirit man by going to church every fourth Sunday, the voice of your spirit is incredibly weak. However, the voice of your body will be loud saying, "Go for it, you can do it!" But, your spirit man is saying softly, "No, no, no." Whichever voice is the most authoritative is the one you will follow. That is why we need to spend more time feeding our spirit. The book of Hebrews talks about God's Word being quick, powerful, and sharper than any two-edged sword. The Word of God is the only tool that can feed the tri-part makeup of a man.

We have to learn to follow the voice of our spirit and teach our young people this too. That is what we do in our youth and children's ministries. We are teaching our children how to follow their spirit. You cannot wait until they get too old. Then it is like trying to teach an adult the alphabet, addition and subtraction. That is something they should have learned as a child. What is happening in many churches today is people who have been attending church for 50 years are just now learning the basics. They still do not understand that they are a spirit. They do not know their alphabet because they have just been attending church and never learning. You will not graduate that way.

A great man of God once said the average

minister dies before reaching the second phase of their ministry because they allow other stuff to get them off course. If that is true for ministers, what do you think about the parishioners? It is safe to say, a very high percentage of saints die before entering the will of God. They simply exist because they have never learned the will of God for their lives. I am not saying this to be cruel. Nevertheless, if you ask the average person, "What has God called you to do?" their response is usually, "I don't know. I went to college and got this degree." Colleges cannot help you find the will of God. You have to go back to the One who created you to find out your purpose. If you wanted to know the purpose of a Hammond organ - what it does or how it works - you would have to go back to the creator or refer to the manual prepared by its maker. Well, it is the same if you are trying to figure out what your purpose is in life. You have to talk to your Creator and refer to His manual, the Bible.

## *Follow the Leading of the Holy Spirit*

The next step to getting "there" is to learn how to follow the leading of the Holy Spirit. You have your human spirit, which is the recreated spirit of man and the Holy Spirit of God. *St. John 16:13* reads, *"Howbeit when He, the Spirit of truth, is come, He will guide (direct) you into all truth: for He shall not speak of himself; but whatsoever He shall hear, that shall He speak: and He will show you things to come."*

Look at *Romans 8:14,* *"For as many as are led by*

*the Spirit of God, they are the sons of God."* You have to be led by the Spirit of God. To be led, you have to learn how to follow. We must learn how to follow the urgings and the promptings of the Holy Spirit. The Holy Spirit will never lead you away from the Word of God. I have heard people say, "The Holy Spirit told me," and it will be something that does not line up with the Word. If the Holy Spirit tells you something, you should be able to find it in the Word because the Holy Spirit and the Word are one. The average parishioner does not know what the Word says because he or she does not read the Bible. A preacher can get in the pulpit and preach on chitterlings and hog maws, and folks will flip over pews and carry on in church because they do not know what the Word says.

Some friends of ours attended a wedding at a supposedly Full Gospel or Word church. They were teaching, in so many words, that it is okay to drink and smoke cigarettes, but stay away from drugs. Well, what is alcohol? It is a substance. Can you imagine a church telling teenagers that it is okay to drink and smoke cigarettes, just stay away from smoking dubs, blunts, and joints. A little social drink or a little wine is okay? How many kids would become alcoholics because they are not going to get just one? They will fire up, drink, and wind up killing a whole family because of drinking and driving.

## *Seek Godly Advice*

Finally, the last step to getting "there" is to seek

godly advice. *Psalm 1* says, *"Blessed is the man that walketh not in the counsel of the ungodly, nor standeth in the way of sinners, nor sitteth in the seat of the scornful."* Be careful about getting counseling from unbelievers because they have wrong intents and motives. You cannot go to just anybody when you are trying to figure out how to get where God wants you to be. Greed may be their motive and you can get yourself in a heap of trouble. I talk with entrepreneurs, wealthy people, all kinds of people, and many of them get into trouble because they seek the counsel of the ungodly. *Proverbs 11:14* says, *"Where no counsel is, the people fall: but in the multitude of counselors there is safety."* You do not need to get in a rush. Remember in *St. Luke 14:28-30*, Jesus talks about building a house without first considering the cost. If you run out of money before it is finished everyone passing by will laugh.

*Proverbs 15:22* reads, *"Without counsel purposes are disappointed: but in the multitude of counselors they are established."* The Hebrew meaning for the word purpose is plan. So without counsel, plans are disappointed. You need godly counsel, a multitude of counselors. You need more than one opinion. Get a second and a third opinion. You do not need to get in a rush. Get some counseling; some good advice.

My ears are always open, especially to those ministers who paved the way, the right way. That is why I listen to Keith Butler, Kenneth Hagin, Fred Price, Oral Roberts, Kenneth Copeland, Lester

Sumrall, T. L. Osborn and John Osteen. I listen to them as godly counsel. What you are getting right now is godly counsel. Of course, godly counsel does not have to come from ministers, but the person should be a proven leader.

There are other godly people. God will give you sisters and brothers in the Lord. He will give you a spiritual mother. You make your choice based on proof. What have they produced? If you need counseling on marriage, do not seek advice from someone who has already had ten husbands or wives. Or if you are looking at starting a business, don't go to someone who has tried ten businesses and all of them failed.

## *Where is Your "There"?*

There is no better place to be than in the perfect will of God. Find out where your "there" is and get there. God will show you His will. Apply what you have read to your life. Pray out the will of God and study and meditate His Word. Follow the voice of your spirit and the leading of the Holy Spirit. Get some godly counseling. Be practical and balanced. Then watch, you'll find yourself knowing where your "there" is; and getting "there" – where God wants you to be will become your sole purpose in life.

# About the Author

Kevin E. Wright is senior pastor of Word of Faith Christian Center in Jackson, Miss. A 1983 graduate of Rhema Bible Training Center in Tulsa, Okla., Wright has worked in full-time ministry for more than 20 years. He served faithfully for over 15 years at Word of Faith International Christian Center in Detroit, Mich., under the leadership of Bishop Keith A. Butler. Wright has established four churches in Mississippi: WOFCC in Vicksburg, Hattiesburg, Yazoo City and Meridian. He is a great advocate for taking the gospel into "every man's world." He is a sought after speaker, empowering people through his line upon line, precept upon precept approach. Kevin lives in the Jackson Metro area with his wife Leslie and five children: Joshua, Stephen, Melissa, Daniel and Micah.

*For information about Word of Faith Christian Center, call (601) 922-9323 or visit www.wofcc-ms.com.*